THE FUNDAMENTAL DUTIES OF PAR

Raising Happy and Responsible Kids: Understanding and Fulfilling Your Core Parental Responsibilities With Ease

BY

NILDA D. MYERS

TABLE   OF CONTENTS.........................PAGES

CHAPTER 1

The Foundations of Parenting.

<u>What is parenting</u>

Parenting is the process of raising and nurturing a child from infancy to adulthood. It involves providing emotional, physical, and social support, guidance, and care to help a child grow and develop into a responsible and well-adjusted individual. Parenting includes various responsibilities such as providing for a child's basic needs, teaching values, setting boundaries, and supporting their education and personal development. It can be a challenging but rewarding journey that plays a crucial role in shaping a child's future.

<u>Parenting also encompasses a wide range of roles and tasks, including:</u>

Emotional Support: Parents offer love, encouragement, and comfort to help their children navigate their emotions and build strong emotional bonds.

Physical Care: This involves meeting a child's basic needs for food, shelter, clothing, and healthcare, ensuring their physical well-being.

Education: Parents are often responsible for their child's early education and play a vital role in fostering a love of learning and curiosity.

Discipline: Setting rules and boundaries, as well as teaching children the difference between right and wrong, is an essential aspect of parenting.

Role Modeling: Parents serve as role models, and their behavior and values often influence their children's attitudes and actions.

Problem-Solving: Parents help their children learn how to solve problems, make decisions, and handle challenges.

Supporting Independence: As children grow, parents gradually encourage them to become more independent while providing guidance and support.

Social Development: Parents help their children develop social skills, empathy, and the ability to build relationships with others.

Safety: Ensuring the safety of their children is a top priority for parents, including teaching them about potential risks and how to stay safe.

Cultural and Moral Values: Transmitting cultural, ethical, and moral values is an important part of parenting, helping children develop a sense of identity and values.

Parenting is a dynamic and evolving process that adapts to a child's changing needs as they progress through different stages of development. Effective parenting involves a balance of love, guidance, and flexibility to help children grow into responsible and confident individuals. It's important to note that there isn't a one-size-fits-all approach to parenting, as each child is unique and may require different forms of support and guidance.

Parenting has several key foundations:

Love and Emotional Support: Providing love, affection, and emotional support is fundamental. Children need to feel secure and valued.

Communication: Open and effective communication helps build trust and understanding between parents and children.

Consistency: Consistent rules and routines provide stability and help children understand boundaries.

Positive Role Modeling: Parents serve as role models for their children, so demonstrating good behavior and values is crucial.

Boundaries and Discipline: Setting appropriate boundaries and using discipline strategies that are fair and age-appropriate is important for teaching responsibility and self-control.

Quality Time: Spending quality time with your children helps build strong relationships and creates lasting memories.

Education and Encouragement: Supporting your child's learning and encouraging their interests fosters growth and development.

Flexibility: Adaptability is key because every child is unique, and parenting styles may need to be adjusted accordingly.

Self-Care: Taking care of your own physical and mental well-being is essential to be the best parent you can be.

Community and Support: Reaching out to support networks, such as family, friends, or parenting groups, can provide valuable guidance and assistance.

Empathy and Understanding: Parents should try to see the world through their child's eyes, understanding their emotions and perspective.

Respect: Showing respect for your child as an individual with their own thoughts and feelings helps build mutual respect.

Safety and Security: Providing a safe and secure environment is essential for a child's physical and emotional well-being.

Independence and Responsibility: Encourage age-appropriate independence and responsibility, allowing children to learn and grow through their experiences.

Problem-Solving Skills: Teach your child how to handle challenges and solve problems, promoting resilience and critical thinking.

Cultural and Moral Values: Instill cultural and moral values that are important to your family, helping your child develop a strong sense of identity and ethics.

Patience: Parenting can be challenging, so patience is vital when dealing with the ups and downs of raising children.

Flexibility in Parenting Styles: Recognize that different children may require different approaches, and be willing to adjust your parenting style accordingly.

Celebrating Achievements: Celebrate your child's successes, no matter how small, to boost their self-esteem and confidence.

Unconditional Love: Let your child know that your love for them is unwavering, regardless of their actions or mistakes.

Teaching Life Skills: Equip your child with practical life skills, such as cooking, budgeting, and time management, to prepare them for adulthood.

Healthy Lifestyle: Promote a healthy lifestyle by encouraging regular exercise, balanced nutrition, and proper sleep.

Conflict Resolution: Teach your child constructive ways to resolve conflicts and handle disagreements with others peacefully.

Encouraging Curiosity: Nurture your child's natural curiosity by fostering their interests and encouraging exploration of new ideas and hobbies.

Adaptability: Be prepared to adapt to the changing needs and interests of your child as they grow and develop.

Responsibility for Actions: Help your child understand the consequences of their actions and take responsibility for their choices.

Time Management: Teach time management skills to help your child balance responsibilities, schoolwork, and leisure activities effectively.

Financial Literacy: Educate your child about money management, savings, and budgeting to instill financial responsibility.

Digital Literacy: In the digital age, guide your child on responsible internet use and online safety.

Parental Unity: If you're parenting with a partner, maintain open communication and a united front when it comes to important parenting decisions and discipline.

Encouraging Creativity: Foster your child's creativity and imagination through activities like art, music, and storytelling.

Teaching Empathy: Help your child develop empathy by encouraging them to understand and care about the feelings of others.

Resilience: Teach your child how to bounce back from setbacks and adversity, promoting emotional strength.

Environmental Awareness: Instill a sense of environmental responsibility and stewardship in your child to care for the planet.

Cultural Diversity: Expose your child to different cultures, traditions, and perspectives to promote tolerance and inclusivity.

Listening Skills: Encourage active listening in your child, which helps them understand others and communicate effectively.

Mindfulness and Emotional Regulation: Teach techniques for managing stress and emotions, like deep breathing or meditation.

Goal Setting: Help your child set and pursue goals, fostering a sense of purpose and achievement.

Conflict Resolution: Show your child healthy ways to resolve conflicts and address issues without resorting to aggression or avoidance.

Gratitude: Cultivate a sense of gratitude in your child by acknowledging and appreciating the positive aspects of life.

Remember that parenting is a dynamic process, and these foundations can adapt to your child's age, personality, and unique circumstances. The key is to provide a nurturing and supportive environment that allows your child to grow into a well-rounded and responsible individual.

CHAPTER 2

Nurturing a Loving Environment During Parenting.

Creating a loving environment during parenting involves:

Unconditional Love: Show your child love and affection consistently, regardless of their behavior.

Communication: Listen actively to your child, encourage open dialogue, and validate their feelings.

Setting Boundaries: Establish clear and age-appropriate rules to provide structure and security.

Quality Time: Spend quality one-on-one time with your child to strengthen your bond.

Positive Reinforcement: Praise and reward good behavior to build their self-esteem.

Empathy: Try to understand their perspective and emotions, fostering empathy in return.

Consistency: Be consistent in your parenting approach and routines.

Model Love: Demonstrate love and respect in your own relationships.

Teach Empathy: Encourage your child to consider others' feelings and needs.

Patience: Understand that mistakes happen and use them as learning opportunities.

Support Independence: Allow your child to make age-appropriate choices, fostering their sense of autonomy and self-confidence.

Physical Affection: Hug, kiss, and cuddle with your child regularly to convey your love physically.

Celebrate Achievements: Recognize and celebrate your child's achievements, no matter how small, to boost their self-esteem.

Manage Your Stress: Take care of your own well-being to be emotionally available for your child.

Forgiveness: Teach the importance of forgiveness and second chances, promoting a forgiving and understanding atmosphere.

Family Rituals: Create family traditions and rituals that reinforce a sense of togetherness and belonging.

Conflict Resolution: Demonstrate healthy conflict resolution skills to show your child how to handle disagreements respectfully.

Read Together: Reading together not only fosters literacy but also provides bonding time.

Encourage Play: Join in your child's play activities to connect on their level and stimulate creativity.

Be a Role Model: Exhibit the behaviors and values you want your child to adopt.

Adapt to Their Needs: Pay attention to your child's changing needs as they grow and adjust your parenting approach accordingly.

Encourage Expression: Support your child in expressing their thoughts and emotions, even if they differ from your own.

Practice Gratitude: Encourage gratitude by discussing the things you're thankful for as a family.

Promote Healthy Lifestyle: Teach the importance of a balanced diet, exercise, and adequate sleep for overall well-being.

Limit Screen Time: Set reasonable limits on screen time to encourage face-to-face interactions and physical activities.

Show Appreciation: Acknowledge your child's efforts and contributions to the family, reinforcing their sense of value.

Maintain Flexibility: While routines are important, be flexible when unexpected situations arise to reduce stress for everyone.

Seek Help When Needed: If you encounter challenges in parenting or family dynamics, don't hesitate to seek guidance from professionals or support groups.

Celebrate Differences: Embrace and celebrate the unique qualities and interests of each family member.

Teach Empowerment: Help your child develop problem-solving skills and resilience to navigate life's challenges.

Create a Safe Space: Ensure your child feels physically and emotionally safe at home, so they can express themselves without fear.

Share Family Stories: Share stories about your family's history and values, passing down traditions and creating a sense of belonging.

Encourage Altruism: Teach your child the joy of helping others through acts of kindness and volunteering.

Celebrate Diversity: Embrace diversity and teach your child to respect and appreciate differences in people from various backgrounds.

Monitor Online Activities: Stay informed about your child's online activities and guide them on responsible internet use.

Celebrate Failures: Encourage a growth mindset by celebrating failures as opportunities for learning and growth.

Plan Adventures: Create opportunities for new experiences and adventures together as a family.

Practice Mindfulness: Teach your child mindfulness techniques to manage stress and cultivate emotional awareness.

Set Realistic Expectations: Avoid pushing your child too hard; instead, set achievable goals and celebrate their progress.

Stay Engaged: As your child grows, maintain your active involvement in their life, showing that your love and support are unwavering.

Remember that parenting is an evolving journey, and there's no one-size-fits-all approach. Adapt these tips to your family's unique dynamics and enjoy the rewarding experience of nurturing a loving and supportive environment for your child's growth and development.

CHAPTER 3

Setting Boundaries and Rules When Parenting.

What is setting boundaries

Setting boundaries refers to establishing clear limits or guidelines for how you allow yourself to be treated by others and how you interact with them. These boundaries can be physical, emotional, or social in nature. Setting boundaries is important for maintaining healthy relationships, protecting your well-being, and ensuring that your needs and values are respected. It involves communicating your limits, saying "no" when necessary, and advocating for your own needs and personal space. Boundaries help maintain a balance between your own priorities and the demands of others, promoting mutual respect and understanding in interactions.

Therefore setting boundaries and rules when parenting is crucial for a healthy and structured family environment.

Here are some tips:

Communicate Clearly: Explain the rules to your children in a simple and age-appropriate manner.

Consistency: Be consistent in enforcing rules. Inconsistency can confuse children.

Age-Appropriate Rules: Tailor rules to your child's age and development stage.

Lead by Example: Children often learn by observing. Be a role model for the behavior you want to see.

Flexibility: While consistency is important, be open to adjustments when necessary.

Positive Reinforcement: Praise and reward good behavior to motivate your child.

Consequences: Establish consequences for breaking rules, but make sure they are fair and appropriate.

Listen Actively: Encourage your child to express their thoughts and concerns. It fosters trust.

Collaboration: Involve your child in rule-setting when appropriate. It can make them feel more responsible.

Monitor and Adjust: As your child grows, rules may need to change to match their evolving needs.

Explain the "Why": Help your child understand the reasons behind the rules. This can make them more likely to follow them.

Encourage Independence: As your child matures, allow them some autonomy in decision-making within the established boundaries.

Family Meetings: Hold regular family meetings to discuss and review rules. It promotes open communication.

Respect Individuality: Recognize and respect your child's unique personality, interests, and needs when setting rules.

Monitor Screen Time: Set limits on screen time and ensure that it doesn't interfere with other important activities like homework and sleep.

Safety First: Emphasize rules related to safety, such as wearing seat belts, using helmets, and stranger danger.

Teach Problem-Solving: Encourage your child to find solutions to conflicts within the boundaries you've set.

Apologize When Necessary: If you make a mistake or overstep, be willing to apologize to your child. It sets a positive example of humility.

Stay Calm: When enforcing rules, maintain a calm and composed demeanor. Avoid yelling or using excessive punishment.

Reinforce Values: Use rules as an opportunity to instill important values like honesty, kindness, and responsibility.

Adapt to Special Needs: If your child has unique needs or challenges, tailor rules and boundaries to accommodate them.

Set Realistic Expectations: Be mindful of your child's capabilities and limitations. Expect age-appropriate behavior and responsibilities.

Gradual Independence: Allow your child to take on more responsibilities as they grow, gradually granting them more freedom.

Prioritize Self-Care: Remember that taking care of yourself is important too. It sets an example of self-respect and balance for your child.

Conflict Resolution: Teach your child healthy ways to resolve conflicts, emphasizing communication, empathy, and compromise.

Stay Informed: Keep up with the challenges and influences your child faces, such as peer pressure, social media, and school activities.

Seek Professional Help: If you're struggling with setting boundaries or managing your child's behavior, don't hesitate to seek advice from a child psychologist or counselor.

Celebrate Achievements: Acknowledge and celebrate your child's successes, both big and small, to boost their self-esteem.

Encourage Hobbies: Support your child in pursuing their interests and hobbies, which can teach them discipline and dedication.

Time Together: Make sure to spend quality time with your child, fostering a strong parent-child bond.

Role Modeling Healthy Relationships: Demonstrate healthy communication and respect within your family, as this will influence how your child interacts with others.

Teach Empathy: Encourage your child to understand and consider the feelings of others, fostering empathy and compassion.

Stay Informed About Friends: Get to know your child's friends and their parents to ensure they have a positive social circle.

Privacy and Trust: As your child grows, respect their need for privacy while maintaining an atmosphere of trust and open communication.

Routine and Structure: Establish daily routines and schedules to provide stability and predictability in your child's life.

Positive Language: Use positive language and reinforcement to encourage good behavior rather than focusing solely on disciplinary measures.

Healthy Eating Habits: Promote balanced nutrition and encourage your child to make healthy food choices.

Limit Materialism: Encourage gratitude and contentment rather than excessive materialism.

Admit Mistakes: When you make a mistake as a parent, admit it and apologize. It teaches humility and accountability.

Stay Involved: Continue to be actively engaged in your child's life as they enter their teenage years, even when they assert their independence.

Setting boundaries and rules in parenting is an ongoing process that adapts to your child's development and changing circumstances. Remember that the primary goal is to provide a safe and nurturing environment for your child to grow, learn, and thrive.

CHAPTER 4

45 Strategies For Effective Communication with Your Child When Parenting.

Effective communication with your child is crucial for building a strong parent-child relationship.

Here are some strategies:

Active Listening: Pay close attention to what your child is saying without interrupting. Show empathy and understanding.

Open and Honest: Be open and honest with your child, age-appropriately, to build trust.

Use Simple Language: Tailor your language to your child's age and comprehension level.

Non-Verbal Communication: Pay attention to your body language and facial expressions; they can convey as much as words.

Empathize: Understand and acknowledge your child's feelings, even if you don't agree with them.

Ask Open-Ended Questions: Encourage conversation with questions that require more than a "yes" or "no" answer.

Set Aside Quality Time: Dedicate time to connect with your child without distractions.

Respect Their Opinions: Even if you disagree, respect your child's opinions and encourage them to express themselves.

Be Patient: Children may take time to express themselves; be patient and let them communicate at their own pace.

Positive Reinforcement: Praise and encourage good communication habits in your child.

Model Good Communication: Demonstrate respectful and effective communication in your own interactions.

Conflict Resolution: Teach problem-solving and conflict resolution skills to help your child express themselves constructively.

Stay Calm: Maintain composure even in challenging conversations; it sets a good example.

Use Stories and Metaphors: Sometimes, using stories or metaphors can help explain complex concepts or emotions to children.

Adapt to Their Needs: Recognize that children's communication needs change as they grow; adjust your approach accordingly.

Limit Screen Time: Excessive screen time can hinder communication; establish screen-free zones or times for quality interaction.

Be Consistent: Consistency in your communication style and rules can provide stability for your child.

Active Participation: Engage in your child's interests and activities. This not only provides opportunities for conversation but also shows your genuine interest in their world.

Avoid Judgment: Encourage your child to express themselves without fearing judgment. Let them know it's okay to make mistakes and learn from them.

Be Mindful of Timing: Choose the right time to discuss important matters. Avoid starting deep conversations when your child is tired or busy.

Use Visual Aids: Younger children may benefit from visual aids like drawings or diagrams to help them express their thoughts and feelings.

Encourage Journaling: Older children and teens can benefit from keeping journals as a means of self-expression. Respect their privacy in this process.

Acknowledge Achievements: Celebrate your child's communication achievements, whether it's speaking up in class or sharing a personal concern.

Stay Informed: Be aware of what's happening in your child's life, including their friends, school, and hobbies, to have relevant conversations.

Address Bullying or Peer Pressure: Discuss topics like bullying and peer pressure to equip your child with strategies to handle such situations.

Apologize When Necessary: If you make a mistake in your communication or behavior, be willing to apologize. It sets a positive example of taking responsibility.

Foster Independence: Encourage your child to make decisions within their age-appropriate abilities. This builds confidence and effective decision-making skills.

Use Technology Wisely: Embrace technology as a tool for communication, but establish rules and boundaries regarding its use within the family.

Seek Professional Help: If you encounter challenges in communication or suspect underlying issues, consider seeking guidance from a child psychologist or counselor.

Celebrate Differences: Acknowledge and celebrate the uniqueness of your child. Embrace their individuality and encourage them to express themselves authentically.

Use Positive Language: Frame your messages in a positive way. Instead of saying "Don't do that," say "Let's try this instead." Positive language encourages cooperation.

Be Mindful of Tone: Pay attention to your tone of voice. A gentle and calm tone can diffuse tense situations and make your child more receptive to what you're saying.

Show Affection: Physical touch, like hugs and pats on the back, can convey love and support when words aren't enough.

Encourage Curiosity: Foster your child's natural curiosity by encouraging questions and exploring answers together. This promotes a love for learning.

Role-Play: Use role-play scenarios to teach your child how to handle different social situations, such as conflict resolution or making new friends.

Teach Empathy: Help your child understand the feelings of others by discussing how different actions might make people feel. Encourage them to consider others' perspectives.

Monitor Your Reactions: Be aware of your emotional reactions. Sometimes, your child might test boundaries or say things to get a reaction. Stay composed and respond thoughtfully.

Set Communication Goals: Work together with your child to set communication goals. This can include improving listening skills or expressing emotions more openly.

Encourage Independence: As your child grows, encourage them to take on more responsibilities and make age-appropriate decisions. This builds confidence and self-esteem.

Seek Feedback: Ask your child how they feel about the way you communicate. Are there things you could do differently to make them feel more comfortable talking to you?

Be Patient with Yourself: Parenting is a learning experience, and effective communication takes time to develop. Don't be too hard on yourself if you face challenges along the way.

Stay Informed About Child Development: Understanding the typical stages of child development can help you tailor your communication approach to your child's specific needs at each age.

Celebrate Achievements Together: When your child achieves milestones or accomplishments, take the time to celebrate together. It reinforces their sense of self-worth.

Promote a Growth Mindset: Encourage your child to see challenges as opportunities to learn and grow. Avoid labeling them or their abilities negatively.

Keep Conversations Balanced: While addressing important topics, ensure that you also engage in light-hearted conversations that simply allow you to bond and have fun together.

Remember that every child is unique, so it's important to adapt these strategies to your child's personality and preferences. Building a strong and open line of communication will not only help you navigate the challenges of parenting but also strengthen your relationship with your child throughout their life.

CHAPTER 5

40 Ways Of Teaching Responsibility and Independence To Your Child As A Part Of Parenting.

Teaching responsibility and independence to your child is crucial for their development.

Here are some effective parenting strategies:

Set Clear Expectations: Clearly communicate your expectations and responsibilities to your child. Make sure they understand what's expected of them.

Role Modeling: Children often learn by observing their parents. Be a responsible and independent role model for them to emulate.

Age-Appropriate Tasks: Assign age-appropriate chores and tasks that gradually increase in complexity as your child grows. Start with simple tasks and gradually add more responsibility.

Positive Reinforcement: Praise and reward your child when they demonstrate responsibility and independence. Positive reinforcement encourages them to continue these behaviors.

Allow Choices: Give your child choices within limits. This helps them learn decision-making skills and independence while still following guidelines.

Problem-Solving: Encourage your child to solve problems on their own. Ask open-ended questions to guide their thinking rather than providing immediate solutions.

Financial Literacy: Teach them about money management, saving, and budgeting. This fosters financial responsibility.

Time Management: Help your child learn to manage their time effectively. Create routines and schedules to instill this skill.

Accountability: Hold your child accountable for their actions and decisions. When they make mistakes, discuss the consequences and encourage them to learn from them.

Encourage Goal-Setting: Teach your child how to set achievable goals and work towards them. This promotes a sense of purpose and responsibility.

Open Communication: Maintain open and respectful communication with your child. Listen to their thoughts and concerns, and provide guidance when needed.

Allow Independence: Gradually give your child more independence as they demonstrate responsibility. This can include managing their own hygiene, homework, and personal space.

Teach Self-Care: Teach your child the importance of self-care, including physical and emotional well-being.

Mistakes Are Learning Opportunities: Emphasize that making mistakes is a natural part of learning and growing. Encourage them to learn from their errors rather than fear them.

Involve Them in Decision-Making: Include your child in family decisions when appropriate. This helps them feel valued and teaches them about making choices that affect the family.

Teach Problem-Solving Skills: Guide your child in solving problems independently. Encourage them to brainstorm solutions and evaluate the outcomes.

Empower Critical Thinking: Encourage critical thinking by asking questions that stimulate discussion and reasoning. This helps them develop analytical skills.

Self-Evaluation: Teach your child to assess their own progress and behavior. Discuss their strengths and areas for improvement, fostering self-awareness.

Respect Their Autonomy: As your child grows, respect their need for privacy and independence while maintaining a safety net of support.

Consistency: Consistency in rules and expectations is vital. Children thrive when they know what to expect and what's expected of them.

Encourage Hobbies and Interests: Support your child in pursuing their interests and hobbies. This can foster a sense of passion and commitment.

Volunteer Together: Engage in community service or volunteering as a family. This teaches empathy, responsibility, and the value of giving back.

Reflect on Values: Discuss family values and ethics with your child. Help them understand the importance of responsibility, honesty, and integrity.

Celebrate Achievements: Celebrate your child's accomplishments, no matter how small. This boosts their self-esteem and motivation.

Gradual Independence: As your child matures, give them more autonomy in decision-making and problem-solving, gradually transitioning to adulthood.

Encourage Self-Advocacy: Teach your child how to express their needs, opinions, and concerns respectfully. This skill is essential for independence.

Time Management Skills: Teach your child how to manage their time effectively by using calendars, planners, or to-do lists. This skill is invaluable for both academic and personal success.

Encourage Self-Discipline: Help your child understand the importance of self-discipline, whether it's in their studies, hobbies, or daily routines.

Problem-Solving Scenarios: Present real-life scenarios and ask your child how they would handle them. Discuss various solutions and their potential outcomes.

Cultivate Empathy: Foster empathy by encouraging your child to consider the feelings and perspectives of others. This helps them build healthy relationships and social responsibility.

Teach Digital Responsibility: In the digital age, educate your child about responsible internet use, social media etiquette, and online safety.

Cooking and Household Skills: Involve your child in meal planning and preparation. Teach them essential cooking and household skills, gradually increasing their responsibilities.

Plan Family Activities: Allow your child to take the lead in planning family outings or vacations, helping them develop organizational and decision-making abilities.

Encourage Reading and Research: Promote independent learning by encouraging your child to read books, explore new topics, and conduct research on their own.

Financial Responsibility: As your child matures, introduce them to concepts like budgeting, saving, and responsible spending. Give them opportunities to manage their allowance or earnings.

Conflict Resolution: Teach your child constructive ways to resolve conflicts and disagreements, emphasizing communication, compromise, and empathy.

Monitor Progress: Regularly check in with your child's progress in developing responsibility and independence. Adjust your guidance as needed.

Positive Affirmations: Continually reinforce your child's self-esteem and belief in their ability to be responsible and independent.

Encourage Leadership: Support your child in taking on leadership roles in school or community activities. This can boost their confidence and sense of responsibility.

Seek Professional Guidance: If you encounter challenges or concerns in your child's development, don't hesitate to seek advice from pediatricians, therapists, or counselors.

Remember that the path to responsibility and independence is a gradual one, and it's essential to adapt your approach to suit your child's unique needs and personality. Encourage them to take ownership of their actions and decisions while providing a supportive and nurturing environment. Ultimately, your guidance will help them become self-reliant and responsible adults.

CHAPTER 6

Encouraging Emotional Intelligence In Your Children During Parenting.

Encouraging emotional intelligence in your children during parenting is crucial for their overall development.

Here are some tips:

Model Emotional Intelligence: Demonstrate how to recognize and express emotions appropriately. Children learn by example, so model empathy, self-awareness, and effective communication.

Open Communication: Create a safe and open environment for your child to express their feelings without judgment. Encourage them to talk about their emotions and listen actively when they do.

Label Emotions: Help your child identify and label their emotions. Use words like "happy," "sad," or "frustrated" to describe feelings, so they can better understand and communicate what they're experiencing.

Teach Problem-Solving: Show your child how to cope with emotions constructively. Discuss various strategies like deep breathing, taking a break, or talking through a problem.

Empathize: When your child is upset, acknowledge their feelings and empathize with them. Say things like, "I can see you're feeling sad; that must be tough." This validates their emotions.

Emotion Stories: Read books or watch shows that explore emotions. Discuss the characters' feelings and how they handle them.

Conflict Resolution: Teach conflict resolution skills, emphasizing compromise and understanding others' perspectives.

Mindfulness and Self-Regulation: Introduce mindfulness exercises to help your child manage strong emotions and improve self-regulation.

Emotion Coaching: Be an emotion coach by guiding your child through their emotional experiences rather than dismissing or punishing them for their feelings.

Set Boundaries: While encouraging emotional expression, establish boundaries for behavior. Help your child understand that while feelings are valid, actions may need to be controlled.

Praise Efforts: Celebrate your child's efforts to manage their emotions and communicate effectively, even if they don't always succeed.

Encourage Empathy: Foster empathy by discussing how others might feel in various situations. Encourage acts of kindness and understanding.

Consistency: Be consistent in your approach to emotional intelligence. Children thrive on routine and predictability.

Positive Reinforcement: Reinforce positive behaviors related to emotional intelligence. Praise your child when they handle emotions well or show empathy towards others.

Problem-Solving Together: When conflicts arise, involve your child in problem-solving discussions. Encourage them to come up with solutions and consider the feelings of all parties involved.

Emotion Vocabulary Expansion: As your child grows, introduce more nuanced emotion words. This can help them express their feelings with greater precision.

Normalize Imperfection: Let your child know that it's okay to make mistakes and experience a range of emotions. Share your own struggles and how you've learned from them.

Social Skills: Teach your child essential social skills like active listening, making eye contact, and using appropriate body language to enhance their emotional intelligence.

Media Literacy: Discuss the portrayal of emotions in media and how it may differ from real-life experiences. Use movies or TV shows as opportunities for conversation about emotional situations.

Encourage Hobbies: Support your child in exploring interests and hobbies. These activities can provide an emotional outlet and help them develop a sense of accomplishment.

Set Realistic Expectations: Recognize that children will have varying emotional development timelines. Don't compare your child's progress to others, and avoid putting undue pressure on them.

Family Time: Spend quality time together as a family. Shared experiences can create opportunities for discussing emotions and building stronger connections.

Seek Professional Help if Needed: If you notice persistent emotional challenges or behaviors that concern you, consider consulting a child psychologist or counselor for guidance.

Self-Care: Model self-care practices for your child. Show them that it's important to take care of one's emotional well-being through activities like exercise, relaxation, and spending time with loved ones.

Celebrate Differences: Encourage your child to appreciate and respect the diversity of emotions and perspectives among people. This fosters inclusivity and emotional intelligence.

Long-Term Perspective: Remember that emotional intelligence is a lifelong skill. Continue nurturing it throughout your child's development, from early childhood to adolescence and beyond.

Reflect and Learn Together: After emotional situations or conflicts, take the time to reflect together with your child. Discuss what happened, how it made everyone feel, and what could be done differently next time.

Encourage Gratitude: Help your child develop a sense of gratitude by discussing things they appreciate and are thankful for. Gratitude fosters positive emotions and empathy.

Volunteer and Give Back: Engage in volunteer activities as a family. This can help your child understand the emotions of those less fortunate and develop empathy and compassion.

Role-Playing: Use role-playing to practice handling emotionally charged situations. This can be especially helpful for teaching conflict resolution and effective communication.

Feedback and Growth: Teach your child that constructive feedback is valuable for personal growth. Encourage them to seek feedback and learn from it.

Be Patient and Consistent: Emotional development takes time, and setbacks are normal. Be patient and consistent in your parenting approach, reinforcing the importance of emotional intelligence.

Encourage Self-Expression: Support your child in finding healthy ways to express their emotions, whether through art, writing, music, or other creative outlets.

Monitor Digital Interaction: In today's digital age, monitor your child's online interactions and help them navigate emotional challenges that can arise in virtual spaces.

Family Meetings: Hold regular family meetings where everyone can discuss their feelings, concerns, and ideas. This fosters a sense of belonging and shared responsibility.

Celebrate Achievements: Acknowledge and celebrate milestones in your child's emotional growth. This reinforces the importance of emotional intelligence in their development.

Seek Professional Guidance: If your child faces significant emotional challenges, don't hesitate to seek professional guidance from therapists or counselors who specialize in child and adolescent emotional development.

Empower Independence: As your child matures, encourage them to make decisions and solve emotional issues independently. Offer guidance but allow them room to grow.

Be a Team: Approach emotional intelligence as a team effort. Let your child know that you're there to support and learn together.

Teach Stress Management: Help your child understand stress and provide techniques for managing it, such as deep breathing, mindfulness exercises, or physical activity.

Normalize Failure: Emphasize that making mistakes is a part of learning and growing emotionally. Share your own experiences of setbacks and how you've overcome them.

Cultivate a Growth Mindset: Encourage a growth mindset by praising effort and perseverance over innate abilities. This mindset fosters resilience and adaptability.

Set Goals Together: Involve your child in setting emotional intelligence goals. Discuss what they'd like to improve and create a plan to work on those areas.

Conflict as Learning Opportunities: Frame conflicts and disagreements as opportunities to learn more about emotions and improve relationships.

Teach Emotional Resilience: Help your child develop emotional resilience by discussing how to bounce back from difficult situations and setbacks.

Empower Decision-Making: As your child matures, involve them in decisions that affect them. This helps them develop autonomy and emotional competence.

Reflect on Media: Discuss the emotional content in movies, TV shows, and video games with your child. Encourage critical thinking about how emotions are portrayed.

Encourage Empathetic Actions: Encourage your child to act on their empathy by volunteering, helping others, or supporting charitable causes.

Celebrate Uniqueness: Emphasize that it's okay to be different and have unique emotional responses. Encourage self-acceptance and respect for diversity.

Be Patient and Supportive: Continue to be a source of emotional support for your child, even as they grow into teenagers and young adults. Offer guidance and a listening ear when needed.

Remember that emotional intelligence is an ongoing process, and there's no one-size-fits-all approach. Adapt your parenting techniques to your child's individual needs and developmental stage. By fostering emotional intelligence from an early age and consistently nurturing it as they grow, you'll equip your child with valuable life skills that will serve them well in relationships, academics, and their overall well-being.

CHAPTER 7

40 Ways Of Handling Discipline and Consequences In your Children.

Handling discipline and consequences for children can be a delicate task.

Here are some effective ways to manage it:

Set Clear Expectations: Establish clear rules and expectations for your children's behavior. Make sure they understand what is acceptable and what is not.

Consistency: Be consistent in enforcing rules and consequences. Children need to know that the same behavior will result in the same consequences each time.

Positive Reinforcement: Encourage good behavior by offering praise, rewards, or privileges when your children follow the rules.

Natural Consequences: Sometimes, allowing children to face the natural consequences of their actions (e.g., not doing homework leads to lower grades) can be a powerful learning experience.

Time-Outs: Use time-outs for younger children to give them a chance to calm down and think about their behavior.

Loss of Privileges: For older children, taking away privileges like screen time, outings, or other activities can be an effective consequence.

Discussion: Have open and age-appropriate discussions with your children about their behavior, the consequences, and why certain actions are not acceptable.

Model Good Behavior: Children often learn by example, so be a role model for the behavior you want to see in them.

Logical Consequences: When possible, impose consequences that are logically related to the misbehavior (e.g., if they break a toy, they may need to help fix it or replace it).

Give Second Chances: Allow children the opportunity to correct their behavior and make amends when appropriate.

Use Empathy: Show understanding and empathy toward your child's feelings and perspective, even when disciplining them.

Avoid Physical Punishment: Avoid physical discipline, as it can lead to negative outcomes and is generally not considered effective.

Time and Patience: Understand that teaching discipline takes time and patience. Be prepared for setbacks and continue to provide guidance.

Seek Professional Help: If you're struggling with discipline issues or if your child's behavior is a concern, consider seeking guidance from a child psychologist or counselor.

Set Realistic Expectations: Keep in mind your child's age and developmental stage when setting expectations. Younger children may not have the same self-control as older ones.

Time and Place: Choose an appropriate time and place for addressing behavioral issues. Avoid discussing problems in front of others, and make sure you have your child's attention.

Stay Calm: It's essential to stay calm and composed when dealing with discipline issues. Losing your temper can escalate the situation and make it harder for your child to understand and learn from their actions.

Avoid Shaming: Focus on the behavior, not the child. Avoid shaming or criticizing your child as a person. Instead, address the specific action that needs correction.

Involve Them in Problem-Solving: Encourage your child to be part of the solution. Ask for their input on how they can avoid similar behavior in the future, which helps them take responsibility for their actions.

Consolidate Lessons: Reinforce the lessons learned from consequences by discussing what they can do differently next time. This helps ensure that discipline serves as a learning opportunity.

Keep Lines of Communication Open: Create an environment where your child feels comfortable discussing their feelings, concerns, or reasons for their behavior. This fosters trust and helps you understand their perspective better.

Monitor Progress: Regularly assess your child's progress in improving their behavior. Celebrate their successes and provide guidance for areas where they still need to improve.

Family Meetings: Hold family meetings to discuss rules, consequences, and behavioral expectations collectively. This can help ensure everyone is on the same page and has a say in family rules.

Be Patient with Yourself: Parenting can be challenging, and you may make mistakes. It's okay to admit when you're wrong and apologize if necessary. Learning and growing together is part of the process.

Seek Support: Don't hesitate to reach out to other parents, support groups, or professionals for advice and emotional support when dealing with challenging discipline situations.

Teach Problem-Solving Skills: Encourage your child to think critically and find solutions to conflicts or challenges. Help them develop problem-solving skills that will serve them well throughout their lives.

Offer Emotional Support: Acknowledge and validate your child's emotions, even when they've misbehaved. Let them know it's okay to feel upset or frustrated but guide them in expressing their emotions in a healthy way.

Set a Routine: Consistent routines can help prevent behavioral issues by providing structure and predictability in your child's life.

Use Positive Language: Frame instructions and feedback positively. Instead of saying, "Don't run," say, "Please walk." Positive language often yields better results.

Praise Effort, Not Just Results: Encourage your child to put effort into their actions and tasks rather than focusing solely on the outcome. Recognize and praise their hard work and perseverance.

Monitor Screen Time: Excessive screen time can lead to behavior problems. Set limits on screen time and ensure it doesn't interfere with other essential activities like homework, chores, or physical activity.

Encourage Independence: Allow your child age-appropriate opportunities for independence and decision-making. This helps them develop a sense of responsibility and ownership over their actions.

Teach Empathy: Help your child understand the impact of their actions on others. Encourage them to consider how others might feel and to treat others with kindness and respect.

Be Flexible: While consistency is important, be willing to adjust rules and consequences when necessary. As your child grows and matures, their needs and challenges may change.

Celebrate Progress: Celebrate small victories and improvements in your child's behavior. Positive reinforcement can motivate them to continue making better choices.

Lead by Example: Demonstrate the values and behaviors you want your child to adopt. Children often mimic the actions of their parents, so modeling good behavior is crucial.

Stay Informed: Keep yourself informed about child development and age-appropriate behavior expectations. This knowledge can help you set realistic goals for your child.

Know When to Seek Professional Help: If your child's behavior consistently poses a danger to themselves or others, or if they show signs of emotional or behavioral disorders, consult with a pediatrician or mental health professional for guidance.

Offer Choices within Limits: Allow your child to make age-appropriate choices whenever possible. This gives them a sense of autonomy and control. For example, you can ask, "Would you like to do your homework before or after dinner?" This empowers them while still adhering to your rules.

Regularly Communicate Values: Have ongoing discussions about your family's values and expectations. Explain the reasons behind rules and consequences, emphasizing how they align with these values. This helps your child understand the purpose of discipline and encourages them to internalize these values.

Effective discipline is a dynamic process that requires patience, adaptability, and continuous learning. Tailor your approach to your child's unique personality and needs, and remember that building a strong parent-child relationship based on trust and love is key to successful discipline.

CHAPTER 8

30 Ways Of Balancing Work and Family Life As a Parent.

Balancing work and family life as a parent can be challenging, but it's essential for overall well-being.

Here are some strategies to help:

Prioritize and set boundaries: Clearly define your work hours and stick to them. Avoid overextending yourself at work, which can cut into family time.

Create a schedule: Plan your day, including both work and family activities. A structured schedule helps you allocate time for both.

Delegate tasks: Share household responsibilities with your partner and involve children in age-appropriate chores to reduce your workload.

Flexibility at work: Explore flexible work arrangements, like telecommuting or flexible hours, if possible. Discuss options with your employer.

Quality over quantity: Focus on the quality of time spent with your family, rather than quantity. Be present and engaged during family interactions.

Learn to say no: Don't overcommit to extracurricular activities or work projects. Prioritize activities that align with your family's values and goals.

Self-care: Make time for self-care to recharge physically and mentally. A well-rested and relaxed parent is better equipped to balance responsibilities.

Communication: Openly communicate with your family about your work commitments and schedule. Ensure everyone is on the same page.

Support network: Seek help from friends, family, or support groups when needed. Don't hesitate to ask for assistance or advice.

Set realistic expectations: Understand that perfection is unattainable. Accept that there will be times when work or family demands more of your attention.

Plan family activities: Schedule regular family outings or activities to create memorable moments and strengthen bonds.

Limit screen time: Encourage limited screen time for both you and your children. Use technology mindfully to maximize quality time together.

Time management: Improve your time management skills. Use tools like calendars and to-do lists to stay organized and prioritize tasks effectively.

Be adaptable: Be prepared for unexpected changes or challenges. Flexibility is key to managing the unpredictable nature of both work and family life.

Seek employer support: Inquire about employer-provided benefits or programs that support parents, such as childcare assistance, parental leave, or employee assistance programs.

Share responsibilities: Communicate openly with your partner about roles and responsibilities, ensuring a fair distribution of tasks both at home and with the kids.

Personal growth: Continue investing in your personal and professional growth, but do so in a way that aligns with your family's needs and goals.

Celebrate achievements: Recognize and celebrate accomplishments, both big and small, both at work and within your family.

Learn to say yes: While it's essential to say no to overcommitment, also learn to say yes to opportunities that align with your long-term family and career goals.

Seek professional help: If you find it increasingly difficult to balance work and family, consider seeking advice from a therapist or counselor who specializes in work-life balance and family issues.

Foster independence: Encourage your children to become more self-reliant as they grow older. Teach them essential life skills to reduce your direct involvement in every aspect of their daily routines.

Plan vacations and downtime: Make sure to schedule regular vacations or breaks where you can disconnect from work and focus entirely on your family. These breaks are vital for rejuvenation.

Set realistic career goals: Consider your family's needs and your career aspirations. Set achievable goals that allow you to progress professionally without sacrificing too much family time.

Evaluate your priorities regularly: Periodically assess your priorities to ensure they align with your family's values and evolving needs. Adjust your commitments accordingly.

Learn stress management techniques: Develop healthy ways to cope with stress, such as mindfulness, meditation, exercise, or hobbies that help you relax.

Be present, not perfect: Strive for presence and connection with your family, rather than trying to be the "perfect" parent. Your presence and love matter most to your children.

Celebrate small wins: Recognize and celebrate your daily accomplishments, no matter how minor they may seem. Small victories can boost your morale.

Seek role models: Connect with other parents who have successfully balanced work and family life. Learn from their experiences and strategies.

Invest in quality childcare: If needed, invest in reliable childcare to ensure your children are well-cared for when you're at work.

Revisit and adjust: Periodically revisit your work-life balance strategies and make adjustments as your children grow and your career evolves.

Remember that every family's situation is unique, and there is no one-size-fits-all solution. What's most important is that you continuously assess and adapt your approach to meet your family's evolving needs while striving for a fulfilling career. Balancing work and family is an ongoing process, and your efforts to maintain that balance will benefit both you and your loved ones.

CHAPTER 9

50 Routes For Supporting Your Child's Education As A Parent.

Supporting your child's education as a parent involves various routes:

Engagement: Stay involved in your child's school life by attending meetings, parent-teacher conferences, and school events.

Communication: Maintain open communication with teachers to track your child's progress and address any concerns.

Homework Routine: Establish a consistent homework routine, providing a quiet and organized space for study.

Encouragement: Praise and encourage your child's efforts and achievements, fostering a positive attitude toward learning.

Reading: Promote a love for reading by having books at home and reading together regularly.

Extracurriculars: Encourage participation in extracurricular activities that align with their interests and talents.

Technology: Use educational apps and websites to supplement learning, but monitor screen time.

Healthy Lifestyle: Ensure your child gets enough sleep, eats healthily, and exercises regularly, as these factors impact learning.

Learning Styles: Understand your child's learning style and adapt your support accordingly.

Limit Distractions: Minimize distractions during study time, such as turning off TVs and phones.

Provide Resources: Invest in educational materials, such as books, art supplies, or educational games.

Set Goals: Work with your child to set achievable academic goals and track progress.

Role Model: Demonstrate a commitment to lifelong learning, setting an example for your child.

Balance: Maintain a balance between academic and non-academic activities to prevent burnout.

Seek Help: If your child struggles with a subject, consider tutoring or extra support.

Stay Informed: Keep up with changes in the education system and curricula.

Emotional Support: Offer emotional support and help your child cope with stress and setbacks.

Encourage Curiosity: Foster a sense of curiosity by answering questions and exploring new topics together.

Respect Independence: As your child grows, encourage them to take responsibility for their learning.

Celebrate Achievements: Celebrate milestones and achievements to boost your child's motivation.

Community Involvement: Encourage involvement in community service or volunteer opportunities, which can enhance their social and emotional development.

Critical Thinking: Promote critical thinking by discussing current events, ethical dilemmas, and problem-solving scenarios.

Time Management: Teach time management skills to help your child balance their academic responsibilities with other activities.

Use Technology Wisely: Help your child develop digital literacy skills and navigate online resources safely.

Build Relationships: Foster positive relationships with peers and teachers, as these can greatly impact a child's school experience.

Financial Literacy: Introduce basic financial concepts and money management to help your child become financially responsible.

Learning Beyond School: Explore educational outings, museums, and cultural experiences to broaden their horizons.

Support Special Needs: If your child has special educational needs, work closely with their school to ensure they receive appropriate support and accommodations.

Encourage Creativity: Allow your child to explore creative outlets like art, music, or writing, which can enhance their problem-solving skills.

Stay Positive: Maintain a positive attitude toward education, emphasizing its importance for their future.

Flexibility: Be flexible and adaptive in your approach, recognizing that your child's needs may change over time.

Respect Their Choices: As they reach adolescence, respect their choices regarding future education and career paths while providing guidance.

Mindful Screen Time: Monitor and regulate your child's screen time, ensuring it aligns with their educational goals and doesn't hinder their learning.

Online Safety: Teach them about online safety, including protecting personal information and recognizing potential online risks.

Stay Informed: Keep up with educational trends and research to make informed decisions about your child's education.

Family Support: Involve other family members in supporting your child's education to create a strong support network.

Cultural Awareness: Promote cultural awareness and diversity by exposing your child to different cultures, traditions, and perspectives.

Conflict Resolution: Teach conflict resolution skills to help them navigate social challenges at school and in life.

Study Skills: Assist your child in developing effective study skills, including note-taking, time management, and test preparation techniques.

College and Career Planning: Start discussing college and career options early, helping them set realistic goals and plan for the future.

Encourage Questions: Encourage them to ask questions and be curious about the world around them. Show that it's okay not to have all the answers.

Stay Organized: Help your child stay organized with school assignments, deadlines, and projects by using planners or digital tools.

Conflict with Teachers: If conflicts arise with teachers or school staff, address them calmly and constructively, modeling conflict resolution skills.

Reflect and Adjust: Periodically review your strategies and adjust your approach as your child's needs evolve.

Positive Reinforcement: Continue offering positive reinforcement and recognition for their efforts, even as they get older.

Community Resources: Explore community resources such as libraries, afterschool programs, and educational workshops.

Mindful Scheduling: Avoid overscheduling with extracurricular activities, ensuring there's enough time for rest and relaxation.

Peer Relationships: Keep an eye on your child's friendships and provide guidance on healthy peer relationships.

Online Research Skills: Teach them how to research effectively online, discern credible sources, and avoid plagiarism.

Self-Evaluation: Encourage self-evaluation and reflection on their progress and areas for improvement.

Remember that your role as a parent is to provide guidance, support, and a safe space for your child to learn and grow. Be patient, adapt to their changing needs, and continue to foster a positive attitude towards education throughout their educational journey.

CHAPTER 10

Fostering Healthy Relationships with Siblings As Part Of Parenting.

Fostering healthy sibling relationships as a parent involves several key strategies:

Promote Communication: Encourage open and respectful communication between siblings. Teach them to express their feelings and listen to each other.

Set Clear Expectations: Establish clear rules and expectations for behavior and conflict resolution. Consistency is crucial.

Conflict Resolution Skills: Teach problem-solving and conflict resolution skills, emphasizing compromise and empathy.

Quality Time: Plan activities where siblings can bond and have fun together, creating positive memories.

Avoid Favoritism: Ensure fairness and avoid showing favoritism, which can lead to jealousy and rivalry.

Encourage Individuality: Respect each child's unique interests and talents, allowing them to develop their identities.

Mediation: Step in when necessary to mediate conflicts, but encourage them to work out minor issues independently.

Model Behavior: Be a positive role model for how to treat others, demonstrating kindness and respect.

Praise and Encouragement: Acknowledge their efforts to get along and praise their positive interactions.

Sibling Bond Building: Help them understand the importance of their lifelong sibling bond and the benefits of a supportive relationship.

Team Building: Encourage siblings to collaborate on tasks or projects, promoting a sense of teamwork and cooperation.

Respect Privacy: Teach them to respect each other's personal space and belongings, fostering a sense of trust.

Avoid Comparisons: Avoid comparing one sibling to another, as this can create resentment and competition.

Celebrate Differences: Emphasize the value of their differences and how they can complement each other.

Problem-Solving Discussions: When conflicts arise, guide them through constructive discussions where they can voice concerns and find solutions together.

Teach Empathy: Help them understand each other's feelings and perspectives, nurturing empathy and compassion.

Family Traditions: Create family traditions or rituals that involve all siblings, reinforcing a sense of togetherness.

Quality Family Time: Spend quality time together as a family to strengthen the overall family bond.

Encourage Independence: Support their individual growth and independence while emphasizing that they can still rely on each other.

Seek Professional Help: If sibling rivalry or conflicts become persistent and harmful, consider seeking guidance from a family therapist or counselor.

Celebrate Achievements Together: Encourage siblings to support and celebrate each other's successes, whether big or small.

Rotate Responsibilities: Assign shared responsibilities, such as household chores or planning family activities, to promote cooperation and shared decision-making.

Family Meetings: Hold regular family meetings where everyone has a chance to voice concerns or suggestions, ensuring each sibling has a say.

Acknowledge Age Differences: Recognize that siblings of different ages may have varying needs and interests, and adjust your parenting approach accordingly.

Sibling Bond Time: Occasionally, arrange one-on-one time between siblings to strengthen their individual connections.

Conflict Debriefing: After resolving conflicts, discuss what was learned and how they can handle similar situations better in the future.

Encourage Empowerment: Teach older siblings to be positive role models and mentors for younger ones, fostering a sense of responsibility and leadership.

Share Family Stories: Share stories about your own experiences with siblings, emphasizing the importance of family bonds.

Supportive Language: Encourage positive language and discourage hurtful comments or name-calling between siblings.

Stay Neutral: In disagreements, avoid taking sides and instead guide them toward finding common ground.

Teach Conflict Resolution Styles: Help your children understand different conflict resolution styles, such as compromise, collaboration, and negotiation, so they can choose the most appropriate approach.

Create Shared Experiences: Plan family outings, vacations, or special events where siblings can create lasting memories together.

Encourage Apologies: Teach them the importance of apologizing when they make mistakes or hurt each other's feelings.

Positive Reinforcement: Recognize and praise their efforts to maintain positive sibling relationships, reinforcing desirable behavior.

Sibling Support Network: Encourage them to turn to each other for emotional support during challenging times, building a strong support network within the family.

Peer Mediation: As they grow older, empower siblings to mediate minor conflicts among themselves, promoting independence and conflict resolution skills.

Role Reversal: Occasionally, let siblings take on roles where they teach each other something they're good at, fostering mutual respect and learning.

Discuss Feelings: Create a safe space for them to express their feelings about their sibling relationship without fear of judgment.

Family Traditions: Establish traditions like regular family dinners or movie nights, providing consistent opportunities for bonding.

Encourage Sibling Creativity: Support their joint creative endeavors, whether it's creating art, music, or writing, as a way to strengthen their connection.

Respect Their Differences: Emphasize that it's okay for siblings to have distinct interests, friends, and talents. Encourage them to celebrate each other's uniqueness.

Conflict Journal: Consider maintaining a "conflict journal" where siblings can write down their feelings about disputes, helping them reflect on and understand their emotions.

Create a Safe Space: Designate a shared area in the home where siblings can spend time together comfortably, like a playroom or a cozy reading corner.

Family Values: Instill family values that promote love, respect, and mutual support, reinforcing the idea that family comes first.

Encourage Sibling Projects: Encourage siblings to work on joint projects, like building a fort, cooking a meal, or gardening, to foster collaboration.

Online Etiquette: Teach responsible online behavior, especially if there are significant age differences, to ensure respectful communication in the digital realm.

Celebrate Sibling Milestones: Acknowledge and celebrate significant events in each sibling's life, such as birthdays, achievements, or milestones.

Outside Support: If necessary, seek guidance from parenting books, workshops, or counselors to help address persistent sibling conflicts.

Sibling Book Club: Start a family book club where siblings read and discuss books together, promoting shared interests and conversations.

Lead by Example: Demonstrate your love and respect for your own siblings or family members, serving as a role model for healthy sibling relationships.

Remember that building and maintaining strong sibling relationships is an ongoing process that evolves over time. Encourage your children to value their siblings as lifelong companions, and provide the guidance and support needed to help them navigate the ups and downs of these important relationships.

Printed in Great Britain
by Amazon